Trees for Life

written and photographed by Nigel Croser

Contents

Introduction	3
Trees and the Environment	4
The Tree-Growing Kit	6
Setting Up	10
The Seedlings	14
Planting Day	20
Index	24

Introduction

It's easy to forget how important trees are to our environment. I wanted to help everyone remember, including myself, so this is what I did.

Trees and the Environment

At school we made a list of ways that trees help the environment. I read the list to my family to help them remember.

1. Trees put oxygen into the air. (We breathe in oxygen.)
2. Trees help stop the world from getting too warm.
3. In some places, trees stop the soil from getting too salty.
4. Trees hold the soil together so rain cannot wash it away.
5. Trees slow down the wind and prevent soil from blowing away. This helps the crops.
6. Trees are places for animals and birds to live and make nests.

5

The Tree-Growing Kit

Next I decided to plant some trees and grow them to help the world. But our yard is not big enough. Dad suggested using a special tree-growing kit. He said that it helps people grow tree seedlings for planting in the community.

The next day Dad went to the store and brought home a kit for growing seedlings. He gave me a list of all the things in the kit. I read it and checked that everything was there.

7

These things were in the kit.
1. a box of soil
2. a packet of plastic tubes
3. a packet of seeds
4. a packet of fertilizer
5. a packet of gravel
6. a book of instructions

Mom helped me read the instructions. Setting up for planting was going to be a big job, so I asked my brother Luke and my friends Dan and Sasha to help me on Saturday.

9

Setting up

We set up the kit on an outside table. We poured all the soil into the wheelbarrow, and I sprinkled it with water.

Then we filled all the plastic tubes with the damp soil and stood them up in the empty soil box. It took a long time, but we had fun.

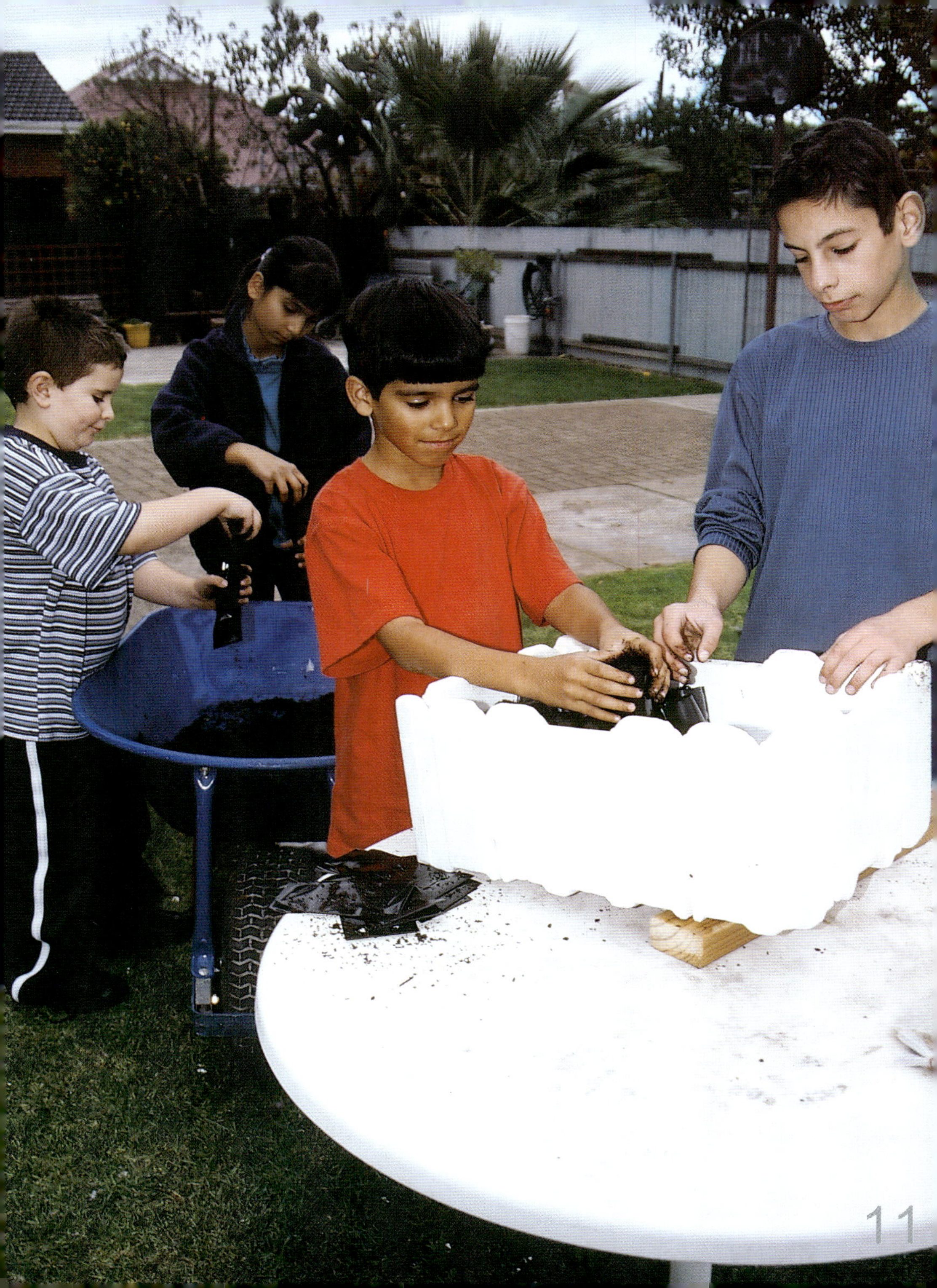

The seeds in the kit were very small. I poured them from the packet onto a saucer. Then we each sprinkled some seeds onto the soil in each tube.

We added some fertilizer and gravel to each tube, too. At last the box was finished. Then we moved the box into a slightly shady place and sprinkled the plastic tubes with water.

13

The Seedlings

After one week the first shoots came up. Each one had two tiny leaves.

Soon the little seedlings had more leaves.

After three weeks there were seedlings in every tube, and we shifted the box to a bright, sunny place.

I did not enjoy the next step. I had to choose the strongest plant in each tube and pull all the others out. The instruction booklet said that this helps make the strongest seedlings even stronger.

I watered the plants every morning before I went to school. I also checked their leaves for insects.

15

When the seedlings were five months old, they were ready to be planted in the ground. I made a timeline to show how they had grown.

week 1
Seeds sprouting

week 2
Seedlings growing

week 3
Put seedlings in sunny place

The red line shows when the seedlings were in the shady place. The green line shows when they were in the sunny place.

week 5

Thin out— leave one seedling in each tube

week 20

Seedlings ready to plant in ground

We had to decide where we wanted to plant our seedlings. Dad suggested that we plant them in the wildlife park. We thought this was a good idea.

We had to get permission to plant our seedlings in the wildlife park. The person in charge of the park said that we could plant them there. I told Luke, Dan, and Sasha, and they said that they would help.

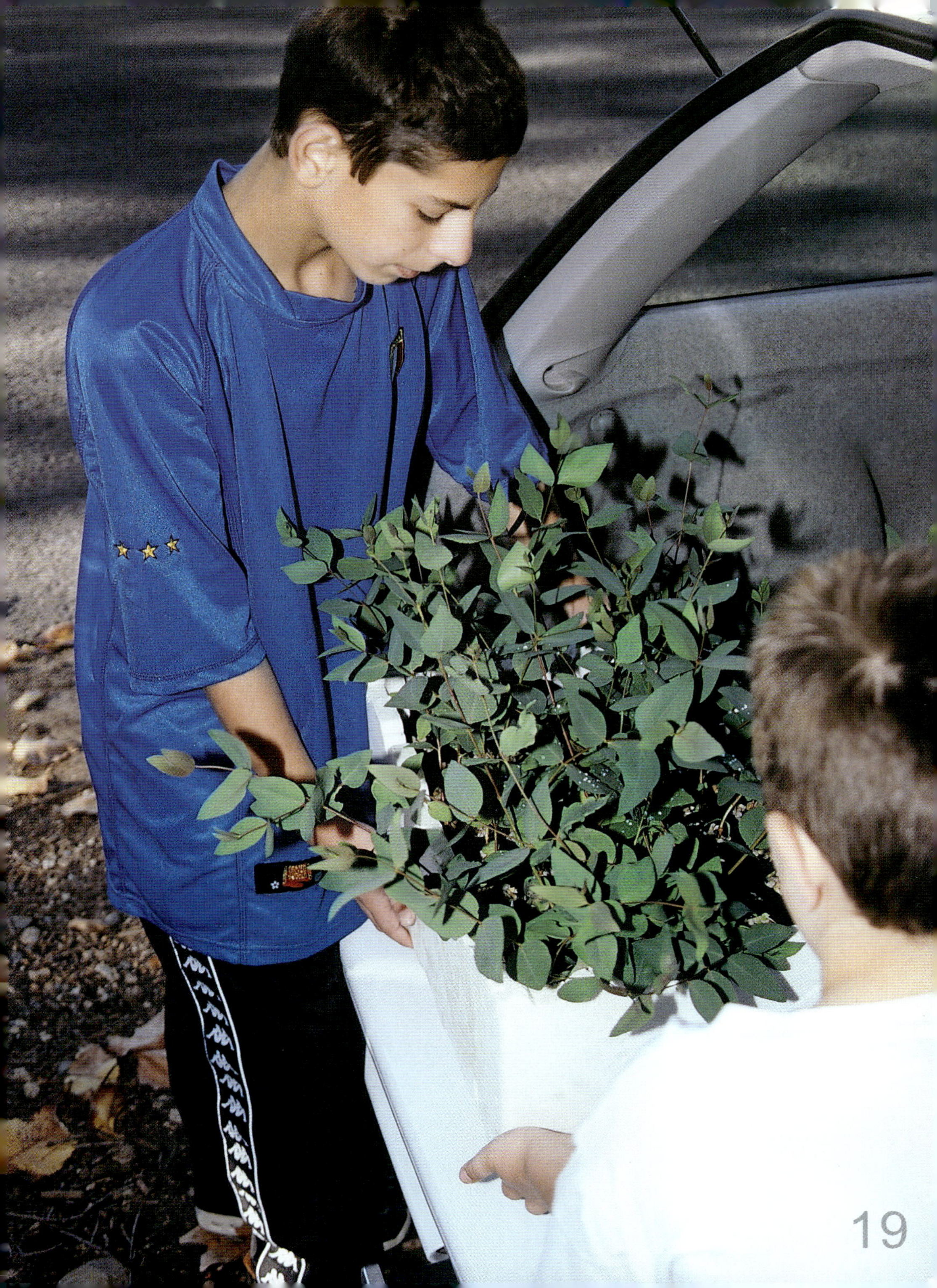

Planting Day

We all got up very early and drove to the wildlife park. Planting the trees was hard work. We had to be careful not to break the seedlings' roots when we took them out of the plastic tubes.

We used buckets to carry water for all the trees. We gave them all a good drink to get them started. We put wire frames around the plants to keep animals away while the trees were small.

Then we made sure that all the empty plastic tubes were picked up so that we did not leave any litter.

21

When we had finished, we went to see the animals in the park. Before we left, we took another look at our little trees. There was a deer nearby. It was a good thing that we had put the wire guards in place!

One day our trees will give shade and shelter to wildlife. We all want to grow more trees next year. I think we should have a setting-up party and invite all our friends over to help!

23

Index

animals 20, 22
box 8, 10, 12, 14
buckets 20
crops 4
environment 3–4
fertilizer 8, 12
gravel 8, 12
ground 16
insects 14
instruction(s) 8, 14
kit 6, 8, 10, 12
leaves 14
litter 20
oxygen 4
permission 18
planted 16
planting 6, 8, 20
plants 20
plastic tubes 8, 10, 12, 20
rain 4
roots 20
salty 4
saucer 12
seedlings 6, 16–18, 20
seeds 8, 12
shade 22
shady 12, 17
shelter 23
shoots 14
soil 4, 8, 10, 12
sunny 14, 17
timeline 16
trees 3–4, 6, 20, 22
water 10, 12, 20
watered 14
wheelbarrow 10
wildlife 22
wildlife park 18, 20
wind 4
wire frames (guards) 20, 22